CU00841850

Idioms for Kids

Cartoons and Fun

INTRODUCTION:
Learning a new idiom a day is a great way to
learn!

Copyright © 2009-2014 Elliot Carruthers

ISBN-13: 978-1499761740
ISBN-10: 1499761740

Let's put "B" on the
back burner. "A" should
be done first.

On the back burner

The back burner refers to the back burner on a stove. A burner is where the flame comes out on top of the oven. Of course... the flame cooks the food. The back burner on a stove is smaller than the front burners. So... food cooks slower on the back burner. It will take more time to cook. It will take longer.

On the back burner = Let's slow it down

Let's use it…

Ok. We can't agree on a color. Let's put it on the back burner.

Ok. We can't agree on a color. Let's get back to choosing a color later.

Ok. We can't agree on a color. Let's put other choices first before the color.

"On the back burner" = Let's decide later
"On the back burner" = Put the choice aside
"On the back burner" = Let's think about it later

Actually. I think you
are skating on thin ice.

Skate on thin ice

Skate refers to ice-skating. If we skate on thin ice... the ice might break and we can fall into the water. So... when you skate on thin ice... you are in danger.

Let's use it…

You should talk nicer to him. You are skating on thin ice.

You should talk nicer to him. You might get in trouble if you make him mad.

You kids are skating on thin ice when you tease the dog.

You kids might get bit when you tease the dog.

Skate on thin ice = you are in danger

I tightened my belt and
saved a lot of money.

Tighten your belt

You tighten your belt when you eat less. Your belt around your belly can get smaller when you buy less food. When you eat less... you spend less money.

Tighten your belt = Spend less money.

Let's use it...

I want to buy a bike so I will tighten my belt.

I want to buy a bike so I will save my money.

Tighten your belt = Saving money

Tighten your belt = Spending less money

I want to save money so I will tighten my belt.

I want to save money so I will spend less.

Tighten your belt = buy less stuff

We can get out of
dodge or we can
blame the cat.

Get out of Dodge

Dodge refers to a famous city from the old west. Dodge was a wild city. Dodge was a lawless city with mean outlaws. A mean cowboy would say... "You better get out of Dodge!" Or... A meek cowboy would say... "I better get out of Dodge!" It was like saying... "This town is not big enough for the two of us. You better get out of Dodge!"

Get out of Dodge = you better get out of here
Get out of Dodge = we should leave
Get out of Dodge = I should go

Let's use it

Uh oh! We broke the vase. We better get out of Dodge!

Uh oh! We broke the vase. We better run!

Here comes the boss. We better get out of dodge.

Here comes the boss. Let's get out of here.

Get out of Dodge = Run!

This shirt makes me
feel fresh as a daisy!

Fresh as a daisy

A daisy is a bright yellow flower with bright white pedals. A daisy has a fresh scent. Fresh means it smells nice and clean. It is a very good smell. When you think of a daisy- think fresh, new and bright. Fresh as a daisy means clean and new.

I ran for miles but I feel fresh as a daisy.

I ran for miles but I feel like I just started.

The shower made me fresh as a daisy because the water felt good.

The shower made me feel new and clean because the water felt good.

Am I tired? No. I feel fresh as a daisy.

Am I tired? No. I feel great.

Fresh as a daisy = I feel clean
Fresh as a daisy = I feel refreshed
Fresh as a daisy = I feel ready to go again
Fresh as a daisy = I have a lot of energy
Fresh as a daisy = I feel great

The jury is
still out.

The Jury is still out.

Juries make decisions in a trial. A jury decides guilt or innocence in a court of law. When the jury is out... it is deciding the verdict. It is deciding the guilt or innocence of a person. The jury goes into a room and talks about the trial. This is called being out. A jury is made of people. So... the people are deciding.

Let's use it...

You made a good sales presentation, but the jury is still out.

You made a good sales presentation, but they are still deciding if they want to buy it.

I think we will move to a new house, but the jury is still out.

I think we will move to a new house, but we have not decided yet.

The Jury is still out = they are thinking about it

The Jury is still out = they have not made a decision yet

The Jury is still out = they will give an answer soon.

You really are a shaker
and a mover! You got
the contract signed!

Mover and shaker

Used as... "They are the movers and shakers". A mover and shaker refers to earthquakes. During an earthquake... the ground moves. The ground moves from side to side. During an earthquake... everything shakes. Trees shake, houses shake, everything shakes. Earthquakes are powerful. Anything that can move and shake is very powerful.

Let's use it....

He is a mover and shaker. He makes all the decisions.

He has the authority. He makes all the decisions.

She is a mover and shaker. She can say yes and buy your product.

She can spend money for the company. She can say yes and buy your product.

Mover and shaker = they are the boss
Mover and shaker = they have the power
Mover and shaker = they can get it done

I knew I shouldn't have counted my chickens before they hatched!

Don't count your chickens before they hatch

You are a chicken farmer... You have chicken eggs and you want to count the chicks in the eggs because you want to sell them. You can't count the chickens in the eggs because some will not hatch. If you only count eggs... you will think you can count on selling more chickens than might come out of the eggs. Don't count something that may not happen.

Don't count your chickens before they hatch = don't rely on something that has not happened yet.

I know you are going to sell your house, but don't count your chickens before they hatch.

I know you are going to sell your house, but it might not sell.

Don't count your chickens before they hatch = don't count on it happening.

I should have added
a stitch. I would have
saved nine stitches.

A stitch in time saves nine

You have a small tear in your shirt. If you put a stitch in it... the tear will not get bigger... ... and you will not need to add more stitches. Of course... a stitch is a small piece of thread used in sewing to join two pieces of clothing together. You use a needle and thread and make a stitch. If a rip starts to happen in your shirt... and you do not add a stitch to hold it... the rip will get bigger. So one stitch saved you from having to put more in. Your roof has a leak and if you do nothing about it- It will get worse.

A stitch in time saves nine = If you do something early about it... it will not get worse.

I see you have a bad tile on your roof. A stitch in time saves nine.

I see you have a bad tile on your roof. You should fix it fast or water will come in and ruin the whole roof.

A stitch in time saves nine = Fix it now or it will be ruined later.

I guess I probably should not give up my day job.

Don't give up your day job

Usually this phrase talks about something that is a hobby. A hobby is something you do for fun but you make no money at it. For example... You paint art but no one pays you. You write books but never publish them. You make songs but never sing them for money. You work at something for fun. So you show your hobby to someone else... and they don't think it's good.

You: What do you think of my painting?
Me: Don't give up your day job
You: Why do you say that?
Me: It's not good art. No one will ever buy it.

Don't give up your day job = It's not good enough to make money.

Don't give up your day job = Don't try to replace your job with this hobby

Don't give up your day job = You won't make money so you will need to keep working

Me: How did you like the book I wrote?
You: Don't give up your day job. I did not like it.

Don't give up your day job = I don't like it

Yes. I have to admit.
It goes in one ear
and out the other.

Goes in one ear and out the other

If something goes in one ear and out the other... ... then it does not stay in your head. If something does not stay in your head... ... you will quickly forget it. This phrase always references spoken words.

I give you advice but it goes in one ear and out the other.

I give you advice but you don't listen to me,

I give you advice but you don't remember it.

Everything I say goes in one ear and out the other. I feel like I am talking to myself.

You ignore everything I say. I feel like I am talking to myself.

Goes in one ear and out the other = you never listen

Yes. You're an eager beaver. You deserve to get a raise.

An eager beaver

Eager beaver describes the actions of a person. Eager means to be enthusiastic and willing. Eager means to be happy to do something. A beaver is an animal. A beaver builds dams and creates a lake so it can catch fish. Beavers are famous for working hard.

Eager beaver = Always ready to work hard

Eager beaver = A person who is happy to work hard

We'll get Bill to work with us because he is an eager beaver.

We'll get Bill to work with us because he is a ready to please and he is hard working.

I am an eager beaver. You can count on me.

I am happy to work hard. You can count on me.

Eager beaver is a compliment

Eager beaver = happy to work hard

The dog was all bark and no bite. He was loud but he would never hurt anyone.

All bark and no bite

A dog that barks- does not always bite. Just because a dog is barking... it does not mean it wants to hurt you. Some dogs bark, but never bite. The dog is loud and scary but harmless. Just like a person could be...

All bark and no bite = Makes a lot of noise but does nothing else.

Don't let the boss scare you. He is all bark and no bite.

Don't let the boss scare you. He yells a lot but that's all he will do.

Don't worry about his mean words. He is all bark and no bite.

Don't worry about his mean words. He acts mean but is actually nice.

All bark and no bite = don't get upset

I studied all night and I burned the midnight oil.

Burn the midnight oil

People used to burn oil in lamps to light up their house at night. So... if you wanted to read at night... you had to burn an oil lamp because light bulbs did not exist yet. If you read late into the night... you will reach midnight. Thus... you burned the midnight oil when you studied at midnight by an oil lamp.

I will get the project done. I will burn the midnight oil.

I will get the project done. I will work all night.

I will pass the test tomorrow. I will burn the midnight oil.

I will pass the test tomorrow. I will study late into the night.

Burn the midnight oil = Work until late

Burn the midnight oil = Study into the night

I invested in giraffes. I don't put all my eggs in one basket.

Don't put all your eggs in one basket

Eggs in this case... means something of great value. Eggs could mean businesses that you own. Eggs could be stocks you own. Eggs in this sentence, usually means something precious and fragile. For example... the egg could mean money or jewelry. The basket means one place. The basket means a location where the valuables are kept.

I only own airline stocks. I put all my eggs in one basket, but I watch the basket well.

I only own airline stocks. It is the only stock I own, but I watch the stocks for changes.

I own many different kinds of businesses. I don't put my eggs in one basket.

I own many different kinds of businesses. I am spread out for safety and one bad business will not put me out of business.

Don't put all your eggs in one basket = Diversify

Sorry but threading
this needle is like
nailing jelly to the wall.

Nailing jelly to the wall

You cannot nail jelly to a wall. Jelly is jam as in - peanut butter and jam. You cannot use a hammer-and-nail to connect jam to the wall. That is impossible.

Nailing jelly to the wall = It is impossible to do.

Nailing jelly to the wall = It cannot be done.

Getting the contract signed is like nailing jelly to the wall.

Getting the contract signed is impossible.

Getting the cat to take a bath is like nailing jelly to the wall.

Getting the cat to take a bath is never going to happen.

Nailing jelly to the wall = It is not doable.

I know it's scraping the bottom of the barrel but this all we have.

Scrape the bottom of the barrel

Barrels were used to hold almost everything in the past. So... when you got to the bottom of the barrel... whatever is in the barrel is almost gone. The barrel is almost empty. If you have to scrape the bottom of the barrel... then there is almost nothing left.

Scrape the bottom of the barrel = there is nothing left

I have one pen left that works. I am scraping the bottom of the barrel.

I have one pen left that works. There are almost no pens left.

I worked all night to come up with a story. I was scraping the bottom of the barrel.

I worked all night to come up with a story. I almost did not think of a story.

Scrape the bottom of the barrel = There is almost nothing left

The boy would soon
discover there was no use
crying over spilled milk.

No use crying over spilled milk

Milk was very rare and valuable a long time ago. So if you spilled it... it was quite a loss. If you spill milk... you cannot drink it... ... so it is lost. If the milk is spilled.... you cannot put it back in the bowl and there is nothing you can do. You lost something valuable and there's nothing you can do about it.

You lost a lot of money. There's no use crying over spilt milk.

You lost a lot of money. Forget about it because it is gone and there is nothing you can do about it.

No use crying over spilled milk = No use crying about bad things that happened

No use crying over spilled milk = Forget it and move on

You look worried. Can I give you a penny for your thoughts?

A penny for your thoughts

A penny bought a lot in the past. For example: One hundred years ago... you could buy an apple with a penny. So... ... a penny had value. If I offer something of value for your thoughts... ... I am saying your thoughts are worth a lot.

A penny for your thoughts = what you think is valuable to me

You look worried- a penny for your thoughts?

You look worried. What you are worried about is important to me.

I need to decide what to do- a penny for your thoughts?

I need to decide what to do. What you think will help me decide.

A penny for your thoughts = Tell me what you think

I cut to the chase and forwarded right to the end of the movie.

Cut to the chase

The chase is the most exciting part of a movie. The movie is boring to watch compared to the chase. The chase refers to any kind of chase. For example... A car chase... a chase with horses... a foot chase. The bad guy is chasing the good guy... or... the good guy is chasing the bad guy. The rest of the movie is boring compared to the chase scene. The chase is the interesting point in the movie.

Cut to the chase = Get to the point
Cut to the chase = Get to the interesting part
Cut to the chase = Please talk about the exciting part

I think your product is interesting. Let's cut to the chase. How much does it cost?

I think your product is interesting. Let's get to the important part. How much does it cost?

Cut to the chase = talk about the most important thing.

I know you say you like me but your actions speak louder than words.

Actions speak louder than words

The "actions" refers to what a person does. The words are what a person says. A person can tell you something. A person can do something other than what they say. For example: A person says: I never eat junk food. Then... You always see them eating junk food. So you say: "I know you say you don't eat bad food, but actions speak louder than words."

Actions speak louder than words = you say one thing and do another

Actions speak louder than words = what you do does not match what you said.

You said I could trust you, but actions speak louder than words because I caught you stealing.

You said I could trust you, but you lied because I caught you stealing.

Actions speak louder than words = you lied about your intentions.

Okay. You have the pen and the ball is in your court. It's up to you to sign the contract

The ball is in your court

This refers to tennis. The ball is in your court when I hit it back to you with my tennis racket. It is now on your side of the court and it is your turn to hit it back. There is nothing I can do, but watch you hit the ball.

The ball is in your court = it is your turn

I finished my part of the report. The ball is in your court.

I finished my part of the report. It's your turn to work on it.

I sent the contract to them. The ball is in their court.

I sent the contract to them. We are waiting for them to sign it.

The ball is in your court = I must wait for you to act now

I know a picture paints a thousand words. This is the ball I was talking about.

A picture paints a

thousand words

You can write words to describe something. Or...
You can draw a picture. It would take many words
to tell what you could just show with a picture. A
picture tells you many different things. For
example: You draw a dog. You can see what kind
of dog it is. You can see what color it is. You can
see how big the dog is. You can see many things
quickly that would take many words to explain.

I can give you the instructions, but a picture paints
a thousand words. Let me get you the blueprints.

I can give you the instructions, but it will be easier
if you see how it is done. Let me get you the
blueprints.

A picture paints a thousand words = It's quicker to
show you.

This has everything
but the kitchen sink.

Everything but the kitchen sink

The kitchen sink is connected to the wall. If you took everything from a house... ...and put it into a truck... ... only the kitchen sink would be left. So... it is a funny way of saying "everything".

What is in the bag? "Everything but the kitchen sink."

What is in the bag? "Too many items to list."

Your room is filled with everything but the kitchen sink.

Your room is filled with a lot of stuff.

Everything but the kitchen sink = A lot of stuff

Everything but the kitchen sink = everything we could think of

Everything but the kitchen sink = tons of items

When I said scarce, this isn't exactly what I had in mind.

Make yourself scarce

Scarce refers to something rare. Scarce means something is hard to find.

Make yourself scarce = be hard to locate

I need to be alone. Please make yourself scarce.

I need to be alone. Please go away.

Make yourself scarce = Please go somewhere else

It looks you are toast my friend.

You are toast

Toast refers to bread baked in a toaster. Toast is the end result of heating bread. Toast is the final result. When it is toast... ... baking is done.

It's toast = It is done

"You are toast" = you are done.

They found the money you stole. You are toast.

They found the money you stole. You're done.

They found the money you stole. You're in big trouble.

You are toast = you are finished.

Pardon my French
but I hit my thumb.

Pardon my French

French refers to the french language. Pardon refers to asking to be forgiven for something you did wrong. You curse by accident. You say a very bad word in front of someone nice. You feel bad about cursing and ask to be forgiven by making fun of it. You pretend the curse word you used... ... was really the french language. You do this because you are ashamed that you said a nasty word.

Dang! Oops. Pardon my French. I did not mean to say dang but I hurt my toe.

Dang! Oops. I just said a bad word. I did not mean to say dang but I hurt my toe.

Pardon my French = sorry I cursed

Pardon my French = I should not have said a bad word

Okay. I may have fallen off
the turnip truck yesterday
but I am not dumb.

Fall off the turnip truck

Turnip refers to a vegetable called a turnip. Vegetables are not smart. Vegetables cannot see or talk. So... A turnip is dumb. If you fall off the turnip truck... ... then you are a turnip... ... and you are dumb. It's often used as... "I did not fall off the turnip truck". Or ... it can be translated as... "I am not a turnip and I am not dumb."

You are trying to trick me. I did not fall off the turnip truck. I am too smart to trick.

You are trying to trick me. I am not dumb. I am too smart to trick.

Fall off the turnip truck = I am not dumb like a turnip

He may look like a babe
in the woods but he sure
can hit a ball.

Babe in the woods

Babe refers to a baby. If a baby is in the woods...
...it cannot defend itself... ...it is in great danger. A baby or a toddler will wander into the woods...
...unaware of the danger.

Babe in the woods = innocent and unaware

He can't be a manager. He is a babe in the woods.

He can't be a manager. He is not experienced enough.

He can't be a manager. He is not mature.

He can't be a manager. He does not know what he is doing.

He can't be a manager. He will make mistakes.

Babe in the woods = Not able to do it because of being too young.

You can teach an old dog a new trick!

You can't teach an old dog a new trick

An old dog can't be trained because it is set in its ways... ...or because it can't learn new things because it is too old... ...or because it has grown stubborn. The idea is... ...when someone already knows how to do something... ... a certain way... ...you cannot teach them a better way because they believe in their old way. Another idea is... ...the old way is not as good as the new way... ...but the person is too foolish to know it.

You can't teach an old dog a new trick = that person will never learn something new

He is not following my instructions. You can't teach an old dog a new trick.

He is not following my instructions. He is too stubborn to learn something new.

You can't teach an old dog a new trick = some people will never learn something new

Okay! Okay! I get your drift!

Get my drift

Drift refers to stuff that floats in the water. Driftwood is an example. Drift moves along with the water. If you get my drift... ... then you are getting what I am sending downstream. It usually refers to something that is said in an implied or secret way... ... said in a way without coming out and saying it... ... like speaking in code.

Get my drift = you are getting what I am sending

Get my drift = you are getting what I am saying

He likes to borrow things and not return them. Do you get my drift?

He likes to borrow things and not return them. Do you know what I mean?

Get my drift = do you understand the secret I am trying to tell you without actually saying it.

Walk a mile in my shoes before
you make comments about how
long it took me to get here.

Walk a mile in my shoes

If you walk in someone else shoes... ...you will know how good their shoes are. So... ...you know how they feel.

Walk a mile in my shoes = experience what I do to know how I feel.

I know you think my job is easy but walk a mile in my shoes.

I know you think my job is easy but do my job and you will understand how hard it is.

I know you think my job is easy but do my job before you decide.

Walk a mile in my shoes = don't judge until you do it yourself

Okay. I'll make a
long story short.

Make a long story short

You can tell a tale and say all the details as you tell it. Then it is a long story. If you skip the small details... ...then you can quickly tell the story. By skipping the unimportant things in the story... ...the time it takes to tell it is short. It took a long time to tell it... ...now it takes a short time. You made the long story become short.

Make a long story short = leave out the small details

I don't have the time now. I'll make a long story short.

I don't have the time now. I'll tell the quick version.

I don't have the time now. I'll tell only the important details.

Make a long story short = cut out the boring stuff.

My ears are burning.
Someone must be
talking about me.

Ears are burning

Burning refers to saying words that are hot. Someone is saying something about you... ...and it is so red hot... ...it makes your ears burn... ...from a great distance. But... here's the catch... they are not saying it in front of you. So... in a magical way... ...your ears burn when someone talks about you... ...but you can't actually hear them. It is based on the superstition that you might sense when someone talks about you from far away.

Ears are burning = someone is talking about me somewhere.

We found you. Were your ears burning? We were just talking about you.

We found you. Did you feel like you were being talked about? We were just talking about you.

We found you. Did you sense our conversation? We were just talking about you.

My ears are burning = I feel someone is talking about me.

Okay. Just tell us where the
money is and you are off the
hook.

Off the hook

Hook refers to a barb on a string. A hook is used to catch fish. The fish is trapped and in trouble. Getting off the hooks means the fish got away.

Off the hook = you got away from trouble.

You're off the hook. They are not going to arrest you.

You're in the clear. They are not going to arrest you.

You're not in trouble. They are not going to arrest you.

You're free to go. They are not going to arrest you.

Off the hook = out of trouble

It's lovely artwork
but it's sort of
hanging by a thread.

Hanging by a thread

Thread refers to sewing thread. Sewing thread is a weak string. It can break because it is so thin. Anything that hangs by a thread... ...can cause the thread to break... ...just by being heavy. When it snaps... whatever is hanging will crash to the ground... ...and possibly break.

Hanging by a thread = it may soon break and fall.

You're hanging by a thread. One more error and you will be in trouble.

You're in great danger. One more error and you will be in trouble.

You're at great risk. One more error and you will be in trouble.

Hanging by a thread = you may soon fail

What did I say about the
contract? I said it's like
shooting fish in a barrel.
Why?

Shooting fish in a barrel

Barrel refers to a wooden barrel or a wooden cask... A cask holds water. If fish are in the water in the barrel and you hunt them... ... it is very easy to catch a fish. You cannot fail. It is not sport and anyone can do it.

Shooting fish in a barrel = it's a sure thing

Shooting fish in a barrel = you can't miss

Selling ices at the beach is like shooting fish in a barrel. Everyone is hot and thirsty.

Selling ices at the beach is very easy. Everyone is hot and thirsty.

Selling ices at the beach is guaranteed. Everyone is hot and thirsty.

Selling ices at the beach is a sure success. Everyone is hot and thirsty.

Shooting fish in a barrel = you can't fail

I think it looks like you have a screw loose.

A screw loose

Screw refers to a screw that holds a machine together. You turn a screw and hold things together. If a screw is loose... ...the machine may not work right because it will shake and break. So... something is wrong with the machine. It is acting wrong. It is acting crazy.

A screw loose = acting crazy.

The cat is jumping all over. It has a screw loose.

The cat is jumping all over. It is crazy.

A screw loose = insane.

Sorry Billy. You can't have
your cake and eat it too.

You can't have your cake and eat it too.

You have a piece of cake. You can eat it... ...or you can save it for later. So... you can eat it or not eat it... ... but you can't do both.

You can't have your cake and eat it too = you can't do both things.

You can play the guitar or the drums but you can't have your cake and eat it too.

You can play the guitar or the drums but you can only play one.

You can't have your cake and eat it too = you have to choose.

Why do I get the feeling you are in cahoots?

In cahoots

"Cahoots" may come from the French word "cahute". Cahute in French means hut. A hut is a cabin or a small house. If you are in cahoots... you are in the hut. If someone is in the hut with you... ...then you become friends. Friends work together. Friends share secrets. Friends become a secret team.

In cahoots = secretly working together.

They are in cahoots. They planned the robbery together.

They are secret partners. They planned the robbery together.

In cahoots = secretly partnered

That's not exactly what I had in mind when I said, "What the doctor ordered".

Just what the doctor ordered

A doctor orders medicine for you... ...medicine is just what you need when you don't feel well. Now you feel better. The doctor tells you what to take... ...that is his order.

Just what the doctor ordered = it's just what I needed.

A cold glass of water is just what the doctor ordered. It's so hot today.

A cold glass of water is what I needed to feel good. It's so hot today.

Just what the doctor ordered = this will be good for me

Just what the doctor ordered = this will make me feel better

It's a secret gift.
Keep it under wraps.

Keep it under wraps

Wraps refers to covering something. We wrap a gift so they won't know what is it is. It keeps everyone from seeing it.

Keep it under wraps = keep it secret

I am writing a new book. Keep it under wraps.

I am writing a new book. Don't tell anyone.

I am writing a new book. Keep it secret

Keep it under wraps = Do not let anyone know about it

I heard your prices
are so good they're a
steal.

A steal

Steal refers to robbing or taking something without paying for it. If you take something and don't pay for it… it's free.

A steal = it is practically free.

That is a good price for the car. It is a steal.

That is a good price for the car. It's almost free.

That is a good price for the car. It's very cheap.

That is a good price for the car. It's like paying nothing.

A steal = so cheap it's practically free

He's here somewhere!
Leave no stone unturned!

Leave no stone unturned

You turn over every stone as you look for something. When all the stones are turned over...
...you looked under them all.

Leave no stone unturned = look everywhere

Find the missing money! Leave no stone unturned!

Find the missing money! Search everything and everywhere

Leave no stone unturned = search all spots

I got a new belt
and now I can
make ends meet.

Make ends meet

"Ends" refers to anything that needs to touch to be completed. For example: You put on a belt and if the ends do no meet... ...the belt won't hold up your pants. If you are building a road... ... it is not complete until both ends touch... ... then the road can be used. So...if you make the ends meet... ... you are a success.

Make ends meet = being successful

Make ends meet = doing well

Make ends meet = making enough money to cover your bills

I got a new job and I can make ends meet.

I got a new job and I make enough money.

I got a new job and I can pay my bills.

Make ends meet = doing well with money

Well. Yes. It is easy
on the eyes but isn't it
a little... bunny-ish?

Easy on the eyes

If something is not easy on the eyes... ...then it is unpleasant to look at. The opposite of easy is difficult or hard. If something is hard to see then it causes you discomfort. If something is easy to see... ...it gives you pleasure. Something or someone that is beautiful... ... pleases you to look at.

Easy on the eyes = pleasing to look at.

The cat is friendly and easy on the eyes.

The cat is friendly and it is pretty.

Easy on the eyes = enjoyable to look at.

Easy on the eyes = beautiful.

Uh-oh! Now you'll have to face the music when the band finds

Face the music

Face refers to turning and looking at something. The music refers to an official marching band... ... like a military band. If you went before a king... official music would play when you approached the throne. If you went before the king... you were likely in trouble.

Face the music = deal with the results of your actions.

I got caught cheating on my report. It's time to face the music.

I got caught cheating on my report. I will have to go before my professor for punishment.

He stole money from the box and they found out. It's time to face the music.

He stole money from the box and they found out. He now has to pay for his actions

Face the music = take the consequences of your action

Face the music = go before someone who will punish you

I used to drop a dime. Now
I have to drop five dollars!

Drop a dime

A dime was the price of a phone call a long time ago. A dime is ten cents or ten pennies. Payphones were the only phones you could use when you were outside. No one had cell phones. You would put a dime in the coin slot... ... and make a phone call.

Drop a dime = make a phone call

Drop a dime = make a call to tell on someone

I found out they are stealing office supplies. I am going to drop a dime.

I found out they are stealing office supplies. I am going to tell someone.

I found out they are stealing office supplies. I am going to let them know.

Drop a dime = tell on someone

Drop a dime = snitch

Drop a dime = inform

Now that I hit the lottery I feel like a million dollars!

Feel like a million

A "million" refers to a million dollars. Having a million dollars is a good feeling. It is very good. "Feel" refers to the way you feel. Do you feel well or do you feel sick.

Feel like a million = I feel very good.

I am doing well. I feel like a million dollars.

I am doing well. My health is very good.

I am doing well. I feel great.

Feel like a million = I am very happy and well

Printed in Great Britain
by Amazon